ACOUSTIC GUITAR

CD songbook 7

ALTERNATE TUNINGS GUITAR COLLECTION

STRING LETTER PUBLISHING

Publisher: David A. Lusterman

Editor: Jeffrey Pepper Rodgers

Music Editor: Andrew DuBrock

Designer: Gary Cribb

Production Coordinator: Judy Zimola

Licensing: Joan Murray

Marketing Manager: Jennifer Fujimoto

Music Transcriptions and Engraving: Andrew DuBrock and Dylan Schorer

Contributors: Alex de Grassi, Andrew DuBrock, Teja Gerken, Niles Hokkanen and Russell Reppert, Jeff Pevar, Jeffrey Pepper Rodgers, Dylan Schorer

Photographs: Paul Brady *(Colm Henry)*, Mary Chapin Carpenter *(Michael Wilson)*, John Cephas and Phil Wiggins *(Tom Radcliffe)*, Sonny Chillingworth *(David Cornwell)*, CPR *(Henry Diltz)*, Alex de Grassi *(Patrick J. Cudahy)*, Ani DiFranco *(Albert Sanchez)*, Peter Finger *(Manfred Pollert)*, Ledward Kaapana *(Paul Schraub)*, Dougie MacLean *(Scotsman Publications)*, David Wilcox *(Michael Wilson)*

STRING LETTER PUBLISHING

contents

introduction

In the last few decades, guitar players of all stripes have been exploring the new world outside of standard tuning (E A D G B E). The simple act of changing these pitches opens a Pandora's box of sounds and possibilities—chords, licks, textures, and techniques that simply aren't possible in standard tuning. Some players use alternate tunings deliberately, knowing that retuning will help them play what they hear in their head in a particular song, while others use tunings specifically so they *don't* know what they're doing—so they can get lost on the fingerboard and happen upon ideas they could never conjure on their own.

The music in this CD songbook provides a unique survey of how contemporary artists are using alternate tunings for both accompaniment and instrumentals. The stellar lineup spans pop/rock (David Crosby with CPR, Ani DiFranco, David Wilcox, Mary Chapin Carpenter), blues (John Cephas and Phil Wiggins), Hawaiian slack-key (Sonny Chillingworth, Ledward Kaapana), fingerstyle (Alex de Grassi, Peter Finger), and Celtic styles (Paul Brady, Dougie MacLean, Trian). You'll hear ten different tunings at work in these songs, a good cross-section of the types of tunings in use today. Take a look at the tuning guide on page 8 to see how these tunings relate to each other and to the basic tuning families.

Learning these songs will surely inspire you to undertake your own experiments with this enticing approach to the guitar. Happy tuner twisting!

Jeffrey Pepper Rodgers
Editor

music notation key

The music in this book is written in standard notation and tablature. Here's how to read it.

STANDARD NOTATION

Standard notation is written on a five-line staff. Notes are written in alphabetical order from A to G.

The duration of a note is determined by three things: the note head, stem, and flag. A whole note (◦) equals four beats. A half note (♩) is half of that: two beats. A quarter note (♩) equals one beat, an eighth note (♪) equals half of one beat, and a 16th note (♬) is a quarter beat (there are four 16th notes per beat).

The fraction (4/4, 3/4, 6/8, etc.) or c character shown at the beginning of a piece of music denotes the time signature. The top number tells you how many beats are in each measure, and the bottom number indicates the rhythmic value of each beat (4 equals a quarter note, 8 equals an eighth note, 16 equals a 16th note, and 2 equals a half note). The most common time signature is 4/4, which signifies four quarter notes per measure and is sometimes designated with the symbol c (for common time). The symbol ¢ stands for cut time (2/2). Most songs are either in 4/4 or 3/4.

TABLATURE

In tablature, the six horizontal lines represent the six strings of the guitar, with the first string on the top and sixth on the bottom. The numbers refer to fret numbers on a given string. The notation and tablature in this book are designed to be used in tandem—refer to the notation to get the rhythmic information and note durations, and refer to the tablature to get the exact locations of the notes on the guitar fingerboard.

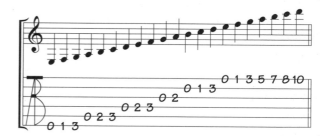

FINGERINGS

Fingerings are indicated with small numbers and letters in the notation. Fretting-hand fingering is indicated with 1 for the index finger, 2 the middle, 3 the ring, 4 the pinky, and T the thumb. Picking-hand fingering is indicated by i for the index finger, m the middle, a the ring, c the pinky, and p the thumb. Circled numbers indicate the string the note is played on. Remember that the fingerings indicated are only suggestions; if you find a different way that works better for you, use it.

CHORD DIAGRAMS

Chord diagrams show where the fingers go on the fingerboard. Frets are shown horizontally. The thick top line represents the nut. A Roman numeral to the right of a diagram indicates a chord played higher up the neck (in this case the top horizontal line is thin). Strings are shown as vertical lines. The line on the far left represents the sixth (lowest) string, and the line on the far right represents the first (highest) string. Dots show where the fingers go, and thick horizontal lines indicate barres. Numbers above the diagram are left-hand finger numbers, as used in standard notation. Again, the fingerings are only suggestions. An *X* indicates a string that should be muted or not played; 0 indicates an open string.

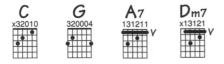

CAPOS

If a capo is used, a Roman numeral indicates the fret where the capo should be placed. The standard notation and tablature is written as if the capo were the nut of the guitar. For instance, a tune capoed anywhere up the neck and played using key-of-G chord shapes and fingerings will be written in the key of G. Likewise, open strings held down by the capo are written as open strings.

TUNINGS

Alternate guitar tunings are given from the lowest (sixth) string to the highest (first) string. For instance, D A D G B E indicates standard tuning with the bottom string dropped to D. Standard notation for songs in alternate tunings always reflects the actual pitches of the notes. Arrows underneath tuning notes indicate strings that are altered from standard tuning and whether they are tuned up or down.

VOCAL TUNES

Vocal tunes are sometimes written with a fully tabbed-out introduction and a vocal melody with chord diagrams for the rest of the piece. The tab intro is usually your indication of which strum or fingerpicking pattern to use in the rest of the piece. The melody with lyrics underneath is the melody sung by the vocalist. Occasionally, smaller notes are written with the melody to indicate the harmony part sung by another vocalist. These are not to be confused with cue notes, which are small notes that indicate melodies that vary when a section is repeated. Listen to a recording of the piece to get a feel for the guitar accompaniment and to hear the singing if you aren't skilled at reading vocal melodies.

ARTICULATIONS

There are a number of ways you can articulate a note on the guitar. Notes connected with slurs (not to be confused with ties) in the tablature or standard notation are articulated with either a hammer-on, pull-off, or slide. Lower notes slurred to higher notes are played as hammer-ons; higher notes slurred to lower notes are played as pull-offs. While it's usually obvious that slurred notes are played as hammer-ons or pull-offs, an *H* or *P* is included above the tablature as an extra reminder.

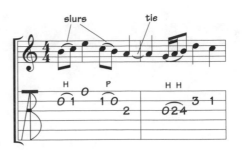

Slides are represented with a dash, and an *S* is included above the tab. A dash preceding a note represents a slide into the note from an indefinite point in the direction of the slide; a dash following a note indicates a slide off of the note to an indefinite point in the direction of the slide. For two slurred notes connected with a slide, you should pick the first note and then slide into the second.

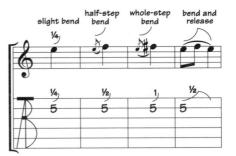

Bends are represented with upward curves, as shown in the next example. Most bends have a specific destination pitch—the number above the bend symbol shows how much the bend raises the string's pitch: ¼ for a slight bend, ½ for a half step, 1 for a whole step.

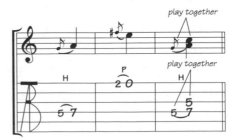

Grace notes are represented by small notes with a dash through the stem in standard notation and with small numbers in the tab. A grace note is a very quick ornament leading into a note, most commonly executed as a hammer-on, pull-off, or slide. In the first example below, pluck the note at the fifth fret on the beat, then quickly hammer onto the seventh fret. The second example is executed as a quick pull-off from the second fret to the open string. In the third example, both notes at the fifth fret are played simultaneously (even though it appears that the fifth fret, fourth string, is to be played by itself), then the seventh fret, fourth string, is quickly hammered.

HARMONICS

Harmonics are represented by diamond-shaped notes in the standard notation and a small dot next to the tablature numbers. Natural harmonics are indicated with the text "Harmonics" or "Harm." above the tablature. Harmonics articulated with the right hand (often called artificial harmonics) include the text "R.H. Harmonics" or "R.H. Harm." above the tab. Right-hand harmonics are executed by lightly touching the harmonic node (usually 12 frets above the open string or fretted note) with the right-hand index finger and plucking the string with the thumb or ring finger or pick. For extended phrases played with right-hand harmonics, the fretted notes are shown in the tab along with instructions to touch the harmonics 12 frets above the notes.

REPEATS

One of the most confusing parts of a musical score can be the navigation symbols, such as repeats, *D.S. al Coda, D.C. al Fine, To Coda,* etc. Repeat symbols are placed at the beginning and end of the passage to be repeated.

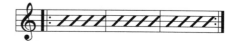

You should ignore repeat symbols with the dots on the right side the first time you encounter them; when you come to a repeat symbol with dots on the left side, jump back to the previous repeat symbol facing the opposite direction (if there is no previous symbol, go to the beginning of the piece). The next time you come to the repeat symbol, ignore it and keep going unless it includes instructions such as "Repeat three times."

A section will often have a different ending after each repeat. The example below includes a first and a second ending. Play until you hit the repeat symbol, jump back to the previous repeat symbol and play until you reach the bracketed first ending, skip the measures under the bracket and jump immediately to the second ending, and then continue.

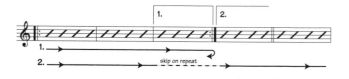

D.S. stands for *dal segno* or "from the sign." When you encounter this indication, jump immediately to the sign (𝄋). *D.S.* is usually accompanied by *al Fine* or *al Coda*. *Fine* indicates the end of a piece. A coda is a final passage near the end of a piece and is indicated with ⊕. *D.S. al Coda* simply tells you to jump back to the sign and continue on until you are instructed to jump to the coda, indicated with *To Coda* ⊕.

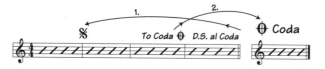

D.C. stands for *da capo* or "from the beginning." Jump to the top of the piece when you encounter this indication.

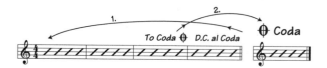

D.C. al Fine tells you to jump to the beginning of a tune and continue until you encounter the *Fine* indicating the end of the piece (ignore the *Fine* the first time through).

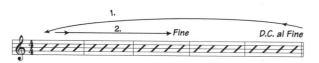

tuning guide

The songs in this book use ten tunings that fall into the basic families shown below. Tunings are written from the sixth string to the first; arrows beneath the notes indicate the strings that are modified from standard tuning, and whether they are tuned up or down.

BASS- AND TREBLE-STRING DROPS

CPR	That House	D A D G B D	Often called double dropped D. Widely used by Neil Young.
Mary Chapin Carpenter	The Moon and St. Christopher	D A D G B C	Close to the "That House" tuning, but with unusual dropping of first string to C.

D TUNINGS

John Cephas and Phil Wiggins	John Henry	D A D F A D	D-minor tuning, much less common than open D major (D A D F# A D).
Trian	The Death of Queen Jane	D A D G A D	Modal version of open D (neither major nor minor), popular in Celtic music.
Peter Finger	101 South	D A E G A D	Like D A D G A D, but with raised fourth string.

G TUNINGS

Sonny Chillingworth Paul Brady	Moe 'Uhane (Dream Slack Key) Arthur McBride	D G D G B D	Open G major. Offers convenient root (G) and fifth (D) on the bass strings.
Ledward Kaapana	Whee Ha Swing	D G D F# B D	G major 7 tuning, known in slack-key parlance as G wahine.

C TUNINGS

David Wilcox Dougie MacLean	Eye of the Hurricane Caledonia	C G C G C E	Open C major. Offers a wide range from low C to high E.

OTHER

Ani DiFranco	Cradle and All	E B B G B D	Open strings form an Em7 chord.
Alex de Grassi	The Water Garden	C G D G A D	Combines elements of open C and D A D G A D; a favorite of Dave Evans and El McMeen.

David Wilcox

For many singer-songwriters, the acoustic guitar is simply an accessible and portable tool for songwriting and performing. But for David Wilcox, perhaps the best known of the brilliant crop of singer-songwriters to emerge in the late '80s, the acoustic guitar is where everything begins. "Songwriting for me is based mostly upon my belief that the guitar knows the song," Wilcox says. "If I listen to the guitar, put it into some weird tuning, and begin to experiment, it plays me a melody."

SELECTED DISCOGRAPHY

Underneath
Vanguard 1173 (1999)

Turning Point
Koch International 7942 (1997)

How Did You Find Me Here
A&M 5275 (1989)

Eye of the Hurricane

Words and music by David Wilcox

David Wilcox kicked off his *How Did You Find Me Here* album with this catchy tune. The version transcribed here is from a live performance for radio station KBCO in Boulder, Colorado. For Wilcox, the guitar setup is relatively tame: open-C tuning (C G C G C E) with a standard capo on the third fret. He strums these chords with a pick, using mainly downstrokes, mutes the strings slightly with his right-hand palm, and accentuates the lower strings throughout. He adds occasional hammer-on and pull-off fills on the fourth and fifth strings

(in a similar fashion as in the intro), but he says the song should be played simply—"The guitar does all the work."

Wilcox wrote "Eye of the Hurricane" a number of years ago, and he later met a young woman who claimed to be the fast-riding spirit he wrote about in the song. The two spent a day together riding their motorcycles, and Wilcox agreed that she is the subject of the song (although, thankfully, she has been spared the unhappy ending).

—Jeffrey Pepper Rodgers

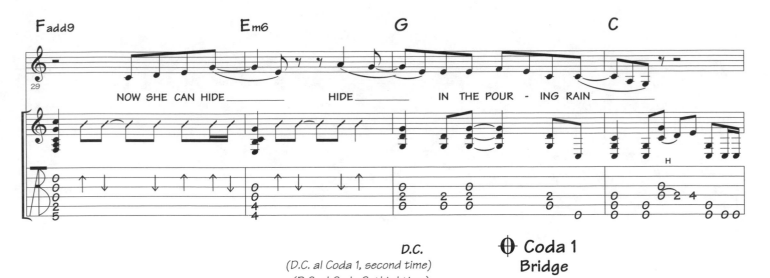

NOW SHE CAN HIDE____ HIDE____ IN THE POUR - ING RAIN____

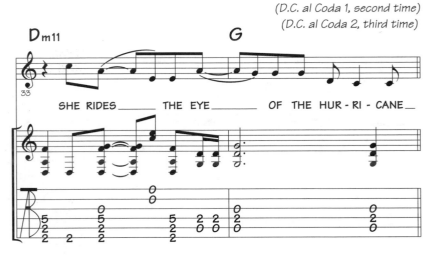

SHE RIDES____ THE EYE____ OF THE HUR - RI - CANE ____

D.C.
(D.C. al Coda 1, second time)
(D.C. al Coda 2, third time)

Coda 1
Bridge

WE SAW HER____

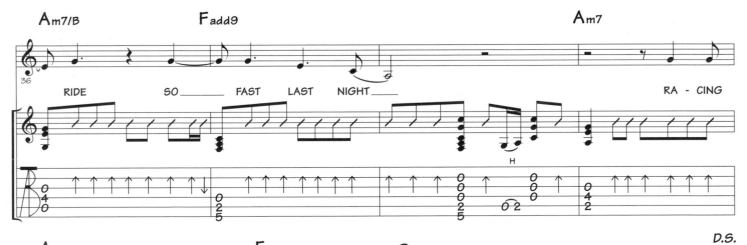

RIDE   SO____ FAST LAST NIGHT____   RA - CING

D.S.

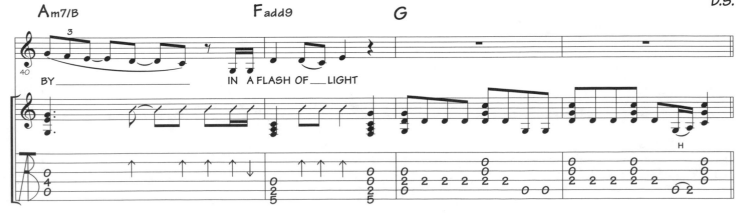

BY_____   IN A FLASH OF____LIGHT

⊕ Coda 2

SHE RIDES ___ THE EYE ___ OF THE HUR-RI-CANE _____ MM _____

MM _____

1. TANK IS FULL, THE SWITCH IS ON
   THE NIGHT IS WARM, COPS ARE GONE
   THE ROCKET BIKE IS ALL HER OWN
   IT'S CALLED A HURRICANE
   SHE TOLD ME ONCE IT'S QUITE A RIDE
   SHE SAID THAT THERE'S THIS PLACE INSIDE
   WHERE IF YOU'RE MOVING YOU CAN HIDE
   SAFE WITHIN THE RAIN

   SHE WANTS TO RUN AWAY
   BUT THERE'S NOWHERE THAT SHE CAN GO
   NOWHERE THE PAIN WON'T COME AGAIN
   NOW SHE CAN HIDE
   HIDE IN THE POURING RAIN
   SHE RIDES THE EYE OF THE HURRICANE

2. TELL THE TRUTH, EXPLAIN TO ME
   HOW YOU GOT THIS NEED FOR SPEED
   SHE LAUGHED AND SAID "IT MIGHT JUST BE
   THE NEXT BEST THING TO LOVE"
   BUT HOPE IS GONE AND SHE CONFESSED THAT
   WHEN YOU LAY YOUR DREAM TO REST
   YOU CAN GET WHAT'S SECOND BEST
   BUT IT'S HARD TO GET ENOUGH

   CHORUS

Bridge
WE SAW HER RIDE SO FAST LAST NIGHT
RACING BY IN A FLASH OF LIGHT

3. RIDING QUICK, THE STREET WAS DARK
   THE SHINING TRUCK SHE THOUGHT WAS PARKED
   HAD BLOCKED HER PATH, STOPPED HER HEART
   BUT NOT THE HURRICANE
   SHE SAW HER CHANCE TO SLIP THE TRAP
   THERE'S JUST THE ROOM TO PASS IN BACK
   BUT THEN IT MOVED, CLOSED THE GAP
   SHE NEVER FELT THE PAIN

   CHORUS
   SHE RIDES THE EYE OF THE HURRICANE, MMM

CPR

The band CPR combines the talents of folk-rock legend David Crosby with ace guitarist Jeff Pevar and Crosby's eldest son, keyboardist/songwriter James Raymond. To date CPR has released a self-titled studio album and a live set that includes new interpretations of several songs made famous by Crosby, Stills, Nash, and Young. Along with Joni Mitchell, Crosby pioneered the use of alternate tunings in pop music, and he continues to use them today to spark ideas for new songs.

SELECTED DISCOGRAPHY

Live at the Wiltern
Samson 148 (1999)

CPR
Samson 145 (1998)

That House

Words by David Crosby, music by Jeff Pevar, David Crosby, and James Raymond

Because we live far away from one other (I live in Connecticut and both James and David live in California), a number of our compositions, including this one, were hatched over time. I had traveled west to write with David and James and was invited to stay on David's boat, *The Mayan*. One morning, as I sat alone on her deck in the harbor playing one of David's guitars, I came up with the acoustic guitar theme that begins the song, which is in double drop-D tuning, with both E strings tuned down a whole step to D. In various writing/arranging sessions, the composition "That House" evolved into the final arrangement that you hear on the *CPR* record. As luck would have it, David's previously composed lyrics fit amazingly well into the instrumental arrangement, and a song was born.

—Jeff Pevar

1. YOU COULD HAVE HEARD A PIN DROP IN THAT HOUSE
   SOMEONE WAS CRYING SOMEWHERE
   INTO A PILLOW THAT IT WASN'T FAIR
   IT GOT LOST SOMEWHERE
   YOU COULDN'T TAKE YOUR HEART OUT IN THAT HOUSE

2. IT JUST MIGHT NOT WANT TO BEAT AGAIN
   A STORM IS POUNDING ON THE ROOF OUTSIDE
   LIKE SOMETHING DIED
   YOU COULDN'T TAKE YOUR HEART OUT IN THAT HOUSE

WATER DRIPPING IN THE SINK
I'M TIRED OF CRYING YOU START TO THINK
THE SOUND LEADS TO THE KITCHEN
THE KITCHEN LEADS TO THE DOOR
AND YOU THINK I MUST NOT LIVE HERE ANYMORE
YOU COULDN'T TAKE YOUR HEART OUT IN THAT HOUSE

CHORUS (3 times)

THEN YOU WALK
WALK ON DOWN TO THE STREET
KEEP ON WALKING

YOU PUT ONE FOOT DOWN IN FRONT OF THE OTHER
(repeat and fade)

Sonny Chillingworth

Sonny Chillingworth (1932–94) was one of the most influential guitarists in Hawaii's captivating slack-key tradition, a bridge between older masters like Gabby Pahinui and next-generation stylists like Ledward Kaapana (who covers Chillingworth's "Whee Ha Swing" in this collection). Chillingworth made his first record in 1954 and continued to play, sing, and compose for four decades, capping his prolific career with two recordings on the Dancing Cat label.

SELECTED DISCOGRAPHY

Endlessly
Dancing Cat/Windham Hill 38027 (1999)

Sonny Solo
Dancing Cat/Windham Hill 38005 (1994)

Moe 'Uhane (Dream Slack Key)

Music by Sonny Chillingworth

This solo guitar piece, recorded on *Sonny Solo,* is a lovely example of how slack-key guitarists use open tunings to create seemingly effortless instrumental textures and melodies. The music came to Chillingworth in a dream—hence the title—and he woke up and captured it on tape in finished form.

Chillingworth takes advantage of every available open string in open-G tuning to let the melody and bass notes ring out—only departing twice in measures 20 and 30, where he barres at the fifth fret. You can play the piece with several different right-hand fingerings, but to emulate Chillingworth's style, plant your ring and pinky fingers firmly on the soundboard and use only your thumb, index, and middle fingers for picking. This formation turns your hand slightly so your middle finger is at more of an angle to the string. Any awkwardness created by this new angle is made up for in stability.

—Andrew DuBrock

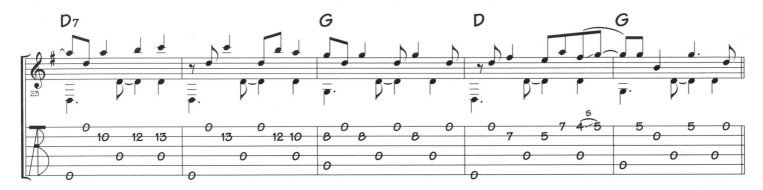

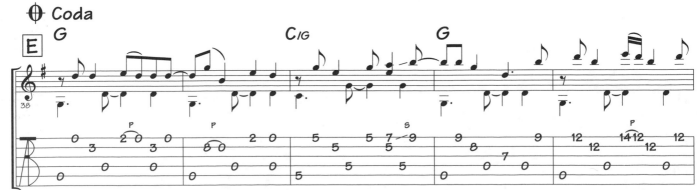

John Cephas and Phil Wiggins

Growing up in the '30s and '40s, John Cephas was always surrounded by music, and learning to play was a natural, organic process. "My first experience with the blues was hearing it when it was played by grownups at house parties," he said. Since then Cephas, along with his partner, harmonica player Phil Wiggins, has become known as one of the prime exponents of Piedmont-style blues, thrilling audiences around the world with his mellow baritone voice and his powerful picking.

SELECTED DISCOGRAPHY

Homemade
Alligator 4863 (1999)
Alligator, PO Box 60234, Chicago, IL 60660;
(773) 973-7736; www.alligator.com

Cool Down
Alligator 4838 (1996)

Dog Days of August
Flying Fish/Rounder 70394 (1983)

John Henry

Traditional, arranged by John Cephas and Phil Wiggins

Although John Cephas plays "John Henry" in the key of D major, he uses the Skip James D-minor tuning (D A D F A D). Cephas opens up with a series of rubato strums over the descending chord shape (played with the second and third fingers). He uses a number of right-hand variations at will throughout the tune. "One time I do it one way, next time . . . it depends on how I feel," Cephas says. "I can hit almost any [right-hand] pattern and it'll be in sync due to the nature

of the tuning. I can hit a six-string chord, I can do two-string pinches. It don't make no difference. All I got to do is put it at the right fret. What you want to do is use a bass and a higher octave or register in order to make it sound really good." Cephas recorded "John Henry" with harmonica player Phil Wiggins on *Dog Days of August*.

—Niles Hokkanen and Russell Reppert

Verse

1. JOHN HEN - RY WAS A LIT - TLE BOY___ (NO) BIG - GER THAN THE
2–9. *See additional lyrics.*

PALM OF___ YOUR HAND   TIME THAT BOY HE WAS

NINE___ YEARS OLD___ DRIV - ING SPIKES LIKE A MAN___

DRIV - ING SPIKES LIKE A MAN___

Guitar Solo

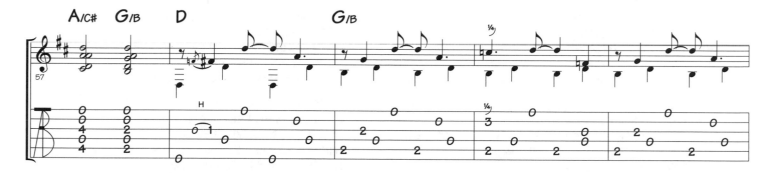

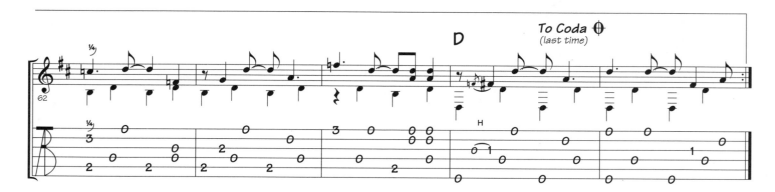

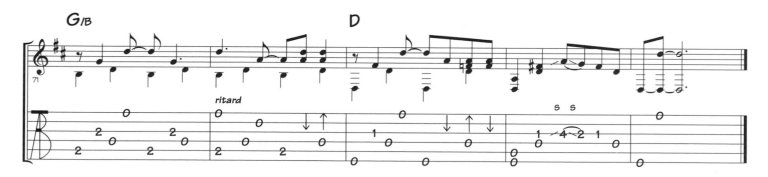

1. JOHN HENRY WAS A LITTLE BOY
    (NO) BIGGER THAN THE PALM OF YOUR HAND
    TIME THAT BOY HE WAS NINE YEARS OLD
    DRIVIN' SPIKE LIKE A MAN
    DRIVIN' SPIKE LIKE A MAN

2. JOHN HENRY WAS A LITTLE BOY
    SITTIN' ON HIS MAMMY'S KNEE
    PICKED UP A HAMMER AND A LITTLE BIT OF STEEL
    HAMMER GONNA BE THE DEATH OF ME
    HAMMER GONNA BE THE DEATH OF ME

3. JOHN HENRY SAID TO THE CAPTAIN, YEAH
    "A MAN AIN'T NOTHING BUT A MAN
    BEFORE I'D LET THE STEAM DRILL BEAT ME DOWN
    I'LL DIE WITH THAT HAMMER IN MY HAND
    DIE WITH THAT HAMMER IN MY HAND"

4. YEAH NOW JOHN HENRY SAID TO THE CAPTAIN, YEAH
    "MAN YOU OUGHT TO SEE ME SWING
    I WEIGH FORTY-NINE POUNDS FROM MY HIPS ON DOWN
    LOVE TO HEAR THAT COLD STEEL RING
    LOVE TO HEAR THAT COLD STEEL RING"

5. JOHN HENRY HAD A LITTLE WIFE
    HER NAME WAS POLLY ANN
    JOHN GOT SICK, LORD HE COULDN'T GET WELL
    POLLY DROVE STEEL LIKE A MAN
    POLLY DROVE STEEL LIKE A MAN

6. WELL NOW JOHN HENRY WENT TO THAT TUNNEL TO DRIVE
    STEAM DRILL WAS BY HIS SIDE
    HE BEAT THAT STEAM DRILL THREE CHESS AND DOWN
    LAID DOWN THE HAMMER, LORD HE DIED
    LAID DOWN THE HAMMER, LORD HE DIED

7. WELL NOW JOHN HENRY DROVE STEEL IN THAT TUNNEL, YEAH
    HAMMER IT CAUGHT ON FIRE
    HE LOOKED AT THE WATER BOY, LORD HE SAID
    "COOL DRINK OF WATER 'FORE I DIE
    COOL DRINK OF WATER 'FORE I DIE"

8. CAPTAIN HE SAID TO JOHN HENRY, YEAH
    "MOUNTAIN IS CAVIN' IN"
    JOHN HENRY SAID, "OH CAPTAIN," YEAH
    "JUST MY HAMMER SUCKIN' WIND
    JUST MY HAMMER SUCKIN' WIND"

9. THEY TOOK JOHN HENRY TO THE GRAVEYARD
    BURIED HIM SIX FEET IN THE SAND
    TIME A LOCOMOTIVE PASS BY
    THERE LIES A STEEL DRIVIN' MAN
    THERE LIES A STEEL DRIVIN' MAN

Ani DiFranco

Ani DiFranco's cut-to-the-chase songwriting, potent stage shows, and ultra-independent stance in the music business have made her one of today's most popular and influential young artists. She debuted in 1990 on her own Righteous Babe label and went on to release no fewer than 13 more albums before the decade's end—in addition to continual performances at ever-larger venues. Her highly sophisticated guitar work makes extensive use of alternate tunings, harmonics, and percussive techniques.

SELECTED DISCOGRAPHY

To the Teeth
Righteous Babe 17 (1999)

Living in Clip
Righteous Babe 11 (1997)

Not a Pretty Girl
Righteous Babe 7 (1995)

Cradle and All

Words and music by Ani DiFranco

Ani DiFranco recorded this powerful song for her 1995 album *Not a Pretty Girl*. The thick, resonant chords in this unique tuning provide an intense backdrop for her melancholy lyrics. She plays most of the chords in the song using the same fingering on the bottom three strings, with the exception of the full barre chords in the bridge, which are played very percussively and with a jagged rhythm. In measure 1, she follows the G chord with a series of rapid-fire hammer-ons and pull-offs on the third and fourth strings. She ends the phrase in measure 2 with harmonics at the 12th and seventh frets. In the fourth verse, the accompaniment drops out entirely and DiFranco's voice comes through like a distant AM radio announcer.

—Dylan Schorer

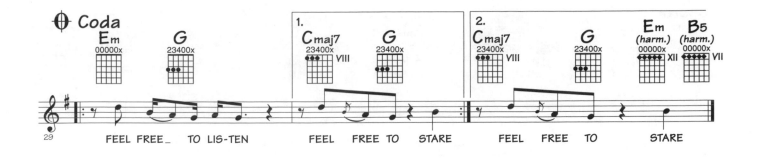

1. FOURTEENTH STREET THE GARBAGE SWIRLS
        LIKE A CYCLONE
    THREE O'CLOCK IN THE AFTERNOON
    AND I AM GOING HOME
    F-TRAIN IS FULL OF HIGH SCHOOL STUDENTS
    SO MUCH SHOUTING SO MUCH LAUGHTER
    LAST NIGHT'S UNDERWEAR IN MY BACK POCKET
    SURE SIGN OF THE MORNING AFTER

        TAKE ME HOME
        TAKE ME HOME AND LEAVE ME THERE
        THINK I'M GONNA CRY, DON'T KNOW WHY
        THINK I'M GONNA SING MYSELF A LULLABY
        FEEL FREE TO LISTEN
        FEEL FREE TO STARE

2. I LIVE IN NEW YORK, NEW YORK
    CITY THAT NEVER SHUTS UP
    IN THE DAYLIGHT EVERYTHING IS SO GORY
    YOU CAN HEAR SNATCHES OF
        STRANGER'S SORRY STORIES
    I MOVED THERE FROM BUFFALO
    BUT THAT'S NOTHING
    THE TRICO PLANT MOVED TO MEXICO
    LEFT MY UNCLE STANDING OUT IN THE COLD
    SAID HERE'S YOUR LAST PAYCHECK
    HAVE FUN GROWING OLD

        CHORUS

Bridge
ROCK-A-BYE BABY IN THE TREETOP
WHEN THE WIND BLOWS THE CRADLE WILL ROCK
WHEN THE BOUGH BREAKS THE CRADLE WILL FALL
AND DOWN WILL COME BABY CRADLE AND ALL

3. YOUTH IS BEAUTY, MONEY IS BEAUTY
    HELL, BEAUTY IS BEAUTY SOMETIMES
    IT'S THE LUCK OF THE DRAW
    IT'S THE NATURAL LAW
    IT'S A JOKE, IT'S A CRIME
    I WAS BORED, YOU WERE BORED
    IT WAS A MEETING OF THE MINDS
    NOW IT'S THREE IN THE AFTERNOON
    AND I CAN'T LEAVE TOO SOON
    SAYING, THANK YOU I HAD A NICE TIME

        CHORUS
        BRIDGE

4. MAYBE I'LL LIVE MY WHOLE LIFE JUST GETTING BY
    MAYBE I'LL BE DISCOVERED
    MAYBE I'LL BE COLONIZED
    YOU CAN TRY TO TRAIN ME LIKE A PET
    YOU CAN TRY TO TEACH ME HOW TO BEHAVE
    BUT I'LL TELL YOU, IF I HAVEN'T LEARNED IT YET
    I AIN'T GONNA SIT, I AIN'T GONNA STAY

        CHORUS

        FEEL FREE TO LISTEN, FEEL FREE TO STARE
        FEEL FREE TO LISTEN, FEEL FREE TO STARE

Alex de Grassi

Alex de Grassi is one of the greatest steel-string guitar player/composers of the last 20 years and a groundbreaker in the use of alternate tunings. His album *Turning: Turning Back,* released in 1978, helped redefine the instrument, combining awesome technique with mature compositional skills. On his 1998 release *The Water Garden,* a collection of solo guitar pieces on the theme of water, de Grassi uses varied tunings to provide new textures and harmonic possibilities.

SELECTED DISCOGRAPHY

Bolivian Blues Bar
Narada Jazz 48282 (1999)

The Water Garden
Tropo 1001 (1998)
Tropo, PO Box 772, Redwood Valley, CA 95470;
www.degrassi.com

Turning: Turning Back
Windham Hill 1004 (1978)

The Water Garden

Music by Alex de Grassi

"The Water Garden" was written to capture the feel of slowly shifting reflections of light on the surface of water. In that spirit, the notes should feel like they are floating and bending over a slow pulse. The C G D G A D tuning allows for some interesting inversions of harmonies you might find in standard tuning. The low string tension and the low C note allow for lots of vibrato and subtle manipulation of pitches that I find very useful in conveying the image of the music. The melody is characterized by long notes linked together by a faster moving countermelody. The melody, and sometimes the bass, often anticipates the downbeat, creating an understated swing or rock ballad feel.

The *X*'s on the noteheads denote slapping the string with the thumb. After the slap, the thumb rests on the string, muting it until it is time to play the next bass note. In measures 4 and 13 the vibrato marking denotes a slow vibrato applied to the whole chord. In measure 10 the right index finger should slap the 19th fret, so as to sound the harmonics of both the open strings and the A (at the seventh fret) along with the fundamental pitches of that part of the chord being held with the left hand. Pay close attention to the note durations and string stops; they will help to clarify the performance.

—*Alex de Grassi*

Like the surface of water...

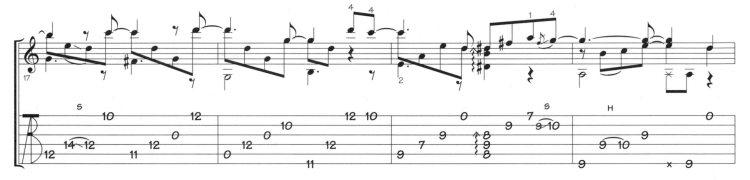

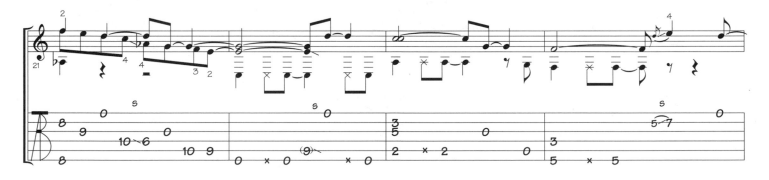

To Coda ⊕

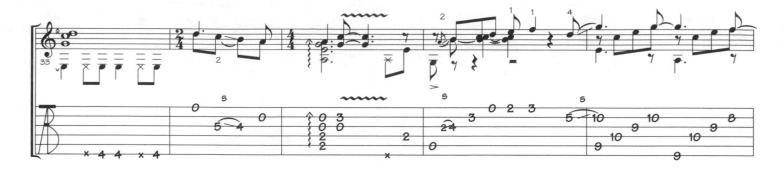

D.S. al Coda

R.H. Slap Harmonics

⊕ Coda

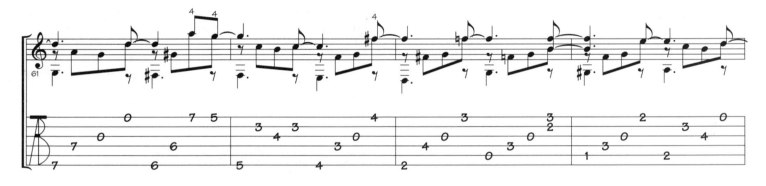

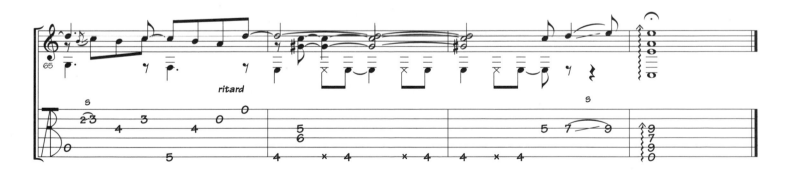

Dougie MacLean

A global ambassador of Scottish music and culture, Dougie MacLean grew up in rural Perthshire, Scotland, the son of a son of a shepherd in the midst of a family with Gaelic Highland origins and a love of melodic, beautiful music. Those early influences haunt his own compositions, which are marked with ancient stories and images and driven by timeless melodies and graceful guitar work.

SELECTED DISCOGRAPHY

Marching Mystery
Blix Street 10062 (1999, originally released in 1994)
Blix Street, PO Box 1129, Burbank, CA 91507;
(800) 851-5825; www.blixstreet.com

The Dougie MacLean Collection
Putumayo 117 (1995)
Putumayo, 324 Lafayette St., 7th Floor, New York, NY 10012;
(212) 625-1400; www.putumayo.com

Craigie Dhu
Dunkeld 001 (1983)
Dunkeld, 4 Cathedral St., Dunkeld, Perthshire PH8 0AW,
Scotland; www.dunkeld.co.uk

Caledonia

Words and music by Dougie MacLean

In the 25 years since Dougie MacLean wrote "Caledonia," this beautiful song has become the unofficial national anthem of Scotland. The performance transcribed here can be heard on his 1983 album *Craigie Dhu* and on *The Dougie MacLean Collection*. Played in open-C tuning capoed at the fourth fret, MacLean's fingerpicked guitar accompaniment is simple but elegant, utilizing graceful pull-offs and emphasizing the contrast between the open fourth-string C and the fifth-string, fifth-fret C. The fingerpicking pattern in measures 5–8 continues through the verses. MacLean overdubbed his own harmony vocals (notated with small notes) in the chorus.

—*Dylan Schorer*

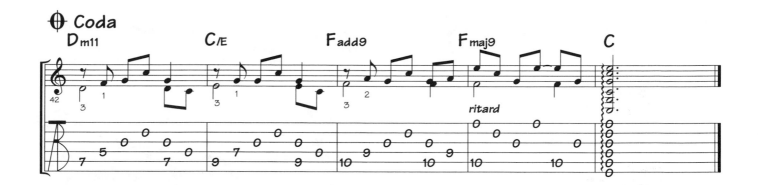

1. I DON'T KNOW IF YOU CAN SEE THE CHANGES
    THAT HAVE COME OVER ME
    IN THESE LAST FEW DAYS I'VE BEEN AFRAID
    THAT I MIGHT DRIFT AWAY
    SO I'VE BEEN TELLING OLD STORIES
    SINGING SONGS THAT MAKE ME
    THINK ABOUT WHERE I CAME FROM
    AND THAT'S THE REASON WHY I SEEM
    SO FAR AWAY TODAY

      LET ME TELL YOU THAT I LOVE YOU
      AND I THINK ABOUT YOU ALL THE TIME
      CALEDONIA, YOU'RE CALLING ME
      AND NOW I'M GOING HOME
      FOR IF I SHOULD BECOME A STRANGER
      YOU KNOW THAT IT WOULD
      MAKE ME MORE THAN SAD
      CALEDONIA'S BEEN EVERYTHING I'VE EVER HAD

2. I HAVE MOVED AND I'VE KEPT ON MOVING
    PROVED THE POINTS THAT I NEEDED PROVING
    LOST THE FRIENDS THAT I NEEDED LOSING
    FOUND OTHERS ON THE WAY
    I HAVE KISSED THE LADIES AND LEFT THEM CRYING
    STOLEN DREAMS, YES THERE'S NO DENYING
    I HAVE TRAVELED HARD
    SOMETIMES WITH CONSCIENCE FLYING
    SOMEWHERE WITH THE WIND

      CHORUS

3. NOW I'M SITTING HERE BEFORE THE FIRE
    THE EMPTY ROOM, THE FOREST CHOIR
    THE FLAMES THAT COULDN'T GET ANY HIGHER
    WELL THEY'VE WITHERED NOW, THEY'VE GONE
    BUT I'M STEADY THINKING, MY WAY IS CLEAR
    AND I KNOW WHAT I WILL DO TOMORROW
    WHEN THE HANDS HAVE SHAKEN
    AND THE KISSES FLOWED
    WELL I WILL DISAPPEAR

      CHORUS

Ledward Kaapana

Ledward Kaapana is one of the masters of Hawaii's indigenous guitar style, slack-key, which uses a wide array of alternate tunings to create gentle rhythms and ringing melodies. Kaapana learned his art from the pioneering players Gabby Pahinui, Ray Kāne, and Sonny Chillingworth (also included in this collection). Kaapana has recorded a number of CDs for George Winston's Dancing Cat series of slack-key recordings and has appeared on a Masters of the Steel-String Guitar tour.

SELECTED DISCOGRAPHY

Waltz of the Wind
Dancing Cat/Windham Hill 38016 (1998)

Led Live
Dancing Cat/Windham Hill 38008 (1994)

Whee Ha Swing

Music by Sonny Chillingworth, arranged by Ledward Kaapana

This showstopper was composed by the late Sonny Chillingworth to test the skills of other slack-key guitarists. The entire tune is made up of five-bar phrases as opposed to four- or eight-bar phrases, which are far more common. This version of the tune, transcribed from Ledward Kaapana's *Led Live* album, shows off some of the flashy licks available in what slack-key players call G-wahine tuning. In mea-

sures 21 and 22, Kaapana continually stops the string with a percussive slap of his right hand, a technique often associated with Chillingworth's playing. "I can always tell it's him when he starts to slap the guitar like an ipu [gourd drum]," Kaapana says of Chillingworth. On *Led Live,* Kaapana performs this piece with his guitar tuned down an additional half step.

—*Dylan Schorer*

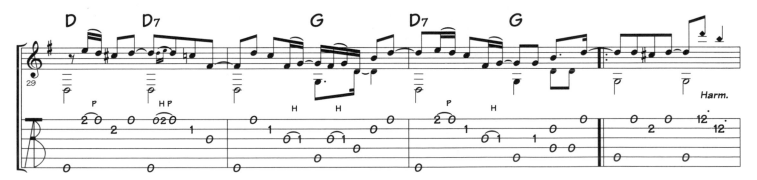

* Slap strings with right hand.

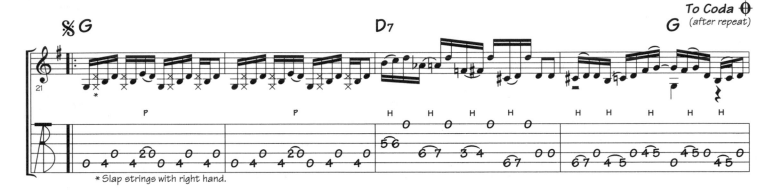

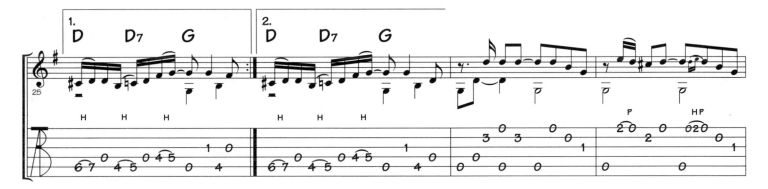

Trian

The Celtic power trio Trian features the guitar playing of Dáithí Sproule, who grew up in Derry, Ireland, listening to B.B. King, Bob Dylan, and Bert Jansch. Sproule's powerful and sensitive guitar work with a variety of tradition-based Celtic artists, including the popular group Altan, has inspired an entire generation of Celtic rhythm guitarists. Like many Celtic players, he favors the modal tuning D A D G A D.

SELECTED DISCOGRAPHY

Trian, *Trian II*
Green Linnet 1159 (1995)
Green Linnet, 43 Beaver Brook Rd., Danbury, CT 06810;
(800) 468-6644; www.greenlinnet.com

Dáithí Sproule, *Heart Made of Glass*
Green Linnet 1123 (1993)

The Death of Queen Jane

Lyrics traditional, music by Dáithí Sproule

This plaintive ballad was first recorded by Dáithí Sproule with the band Skara Brae. Probably the best-known version was recorded by the Bothy Band on *After Hours* (Green Linnet). The version shown here was taken from the 1995 album *Trian II* by the group Trian, which features Sproule on guitar, Liz Carroll on fiddle, and Billy McComiskey on accordion. The words, about the death of one of Henry VIII's wives, were discovered by Sproule in a book and put to music in 1970 or '71. The guitar introduction and accompaniment exemplifies the graceful beauty easily available in D A D G A D tuning and the rich chords it affords. The fingerpicking pattern shown in measure 1 of the introduction is similar to the pattern used for the various chords throughout the verses.

—Dylan Schorer

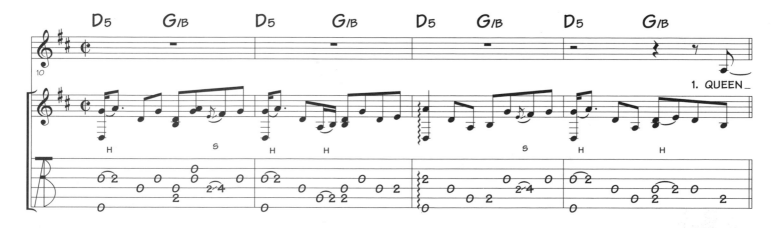

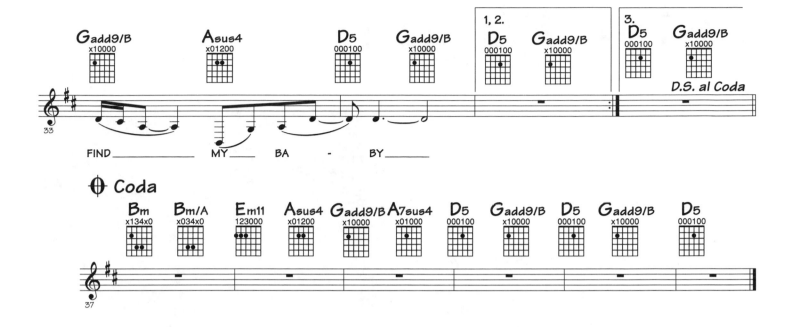

Coda

1. QUEEN JANE LAY IN LABOR
   FULL NINE DAYS OR MORE
   TILL THE WOMAN GREW SO TIRED
   THEY COULD NO LONGER THERE
   THEY COULD NO LONGER THERE

2. "GOOD WOMEN, GOOD WOMEN
   GOOD WOMEN AS YE BE
   WILL YOU OPEN UP MY RIGHT SIDE
   AND FIND MY BABY
   AND FIND MY BABY"

3. "OH, NO," CRIED THE WOMEN
   "THAT NEVER MAY BE
   WE WILL SEND FOR KING HENRY
   AND HEAR WHAT HE MAY SAY
   AND HEAR WHAT HE MAY SAY"

   INSTRUMENTAL

4. KING HENRY WAS SENT FOR
   AND KING HENRY DID COME
   SAYING, "WHAT DO AIL YOU MY LADY?
   YOUR EYES THEY LOOK SO DIM
   YOUR EYES THEY LOOK SO DIM"

5. "KING HENRY, KING HENRY
   WILL YOU DO ONE THING FOR ME?
   THAT'S TO OPEN MY RIGHT SIDE
   AND FIND MY BABY
   AND FIND MY BABY"

6. "OH, NO" CRIED KING HENRY
   "THAT'S A THING I WOULD NEVER DO
   FOR IF I LOSE THE FLOWER OF ENGLAND
   I SHALL LOSE THE BRANCH TOO
   I SHALL LOSE THE BRANCH TOO"

7. THERE WAS FIDDLING
   AYE, AND DANCING
   ON THE DAY THE BABE WAS BORN
   BUT POOR QUEEN JANE, BELOVED
   LAY COLD AS A STONE
   LAY COLD AS A STONE

   INSTRUMENTAL

Peter Finger

Peter Finger's solo guitar work isn't widely known in the U.S., but those lucky enough to discover him are astounded by the power and precision of his playing and the depth of his compositions. Finger began recording and releasing albums on his own label, Acoustic Music Records, in 1989. His 1999 release *Open Strings* is a master-piece of melody, texture, and rhythm.

SELECTED DISCOGRAPHY

Open Strings
Acoustic Music 1173 (1999)
Acoustic Music, Postfach 1945, 49009 Osnabrück, Germany;
fax (49) 541-70-86-67; www.acoustic-music.de

Best of Peter Finger and Florian Poser
Acoustic Music 1140 (1997)

Between the Lines
Acoustic Music 1079 (1995)

101 South

Music by Peter Finger

Peter Finger's CD *Open Strings* includes "101 South," the melodic and challenging solo piece transcribed below. He named the piece while touring in California. Finger had never been comfortable in standard tuning and chose E B E G A D as his main tuning after a tour with French fingerstylist Pierre Bensusan, who had just started to use D A D G A D exclusively. Finger recalls, "I worked out all the harmonies, scales, chords, everything I wanted to know. I realized that you could do enough with that one tuning." Ultimately, Finger ended up settling on two tunings: E B E G A D and a variation with the fifth and sixth strings tuned down a whole step—D A E G A D.

Finger notes that when playing "101 South," it's helpful to realize that the tune is based more on chords than on single-note lines. He warns that the biggest challenges are keeping the melody fluid while making considerable jumps around the fingerboard and getting the rhythm right. He recommends slowing down to a comfortable tempo and using a metronome while working out the various parts.

—Teja Gerken

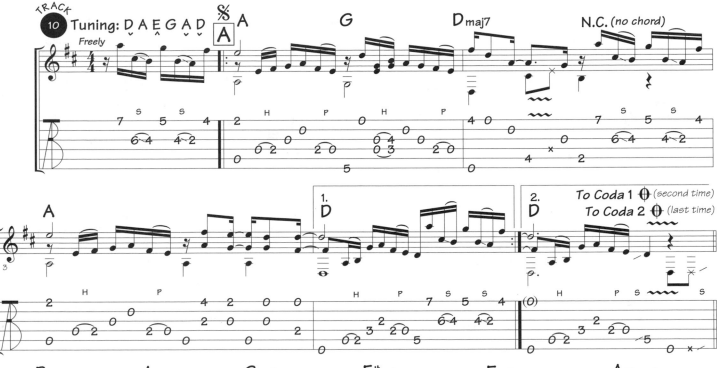

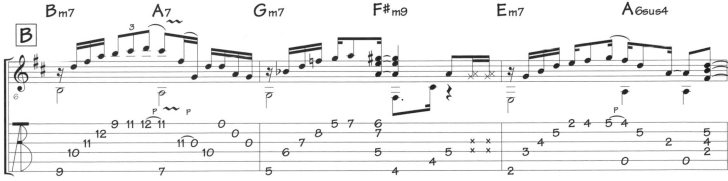

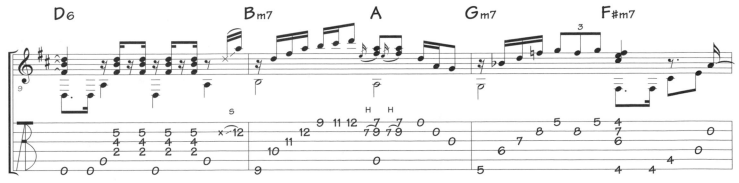

Coda 2

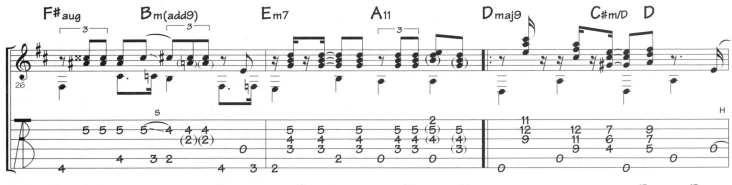

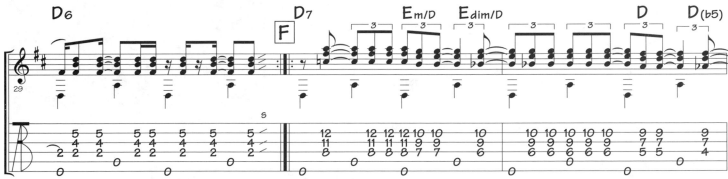

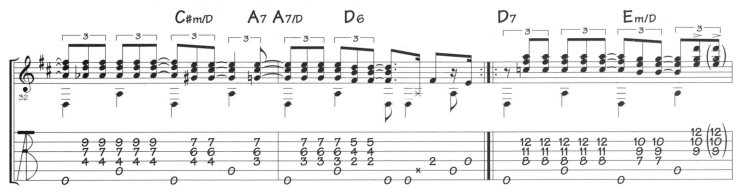

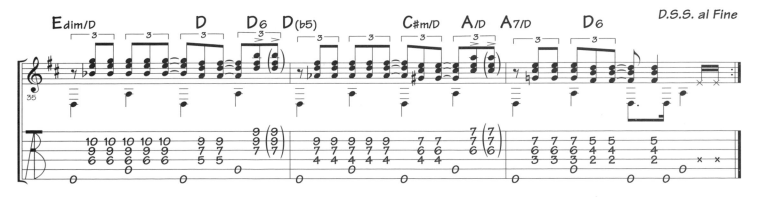

Mary Chapin Carpenter

Real life—with all its jagged edges, less-than-perfect players, and unhappy end-ings—reverberates clearly in Mary Chapin Carpenter's songs. With a bracing mix of sharply focused, day-in-the-life imagery and a down-to-earth performance style, Carpenter has won legions of fans and watched her seven albums climb the country charts. Particularly on her ballads, she often achieves subtle effects by altering one or more strings from standard tuning.

The Moon and St. Christopher

Words and music by Mary Chapin Carpenter

Mary Chapin Carpenter's unusual tuning for this quiet ballad, recorded on *Shooting Straight in the Dark,* leaves the first and second strings a half step apart. So when she fingers the second string on the first fret above the capo, the top two strings are in unison. Carpenter fingerpicks and arpeggiates the chords, sometimes ending measures

of C and F with the open second string. Her slow arpeggios allow her to use the open first string as a kind of drone without changing the harmonies or creating too much dissonance with the second string. Carpenter's longtime musical partner, guitarist John Jennings, plays the solo in bars 41–49.

—*Jeffrey Pepper Rodgers*

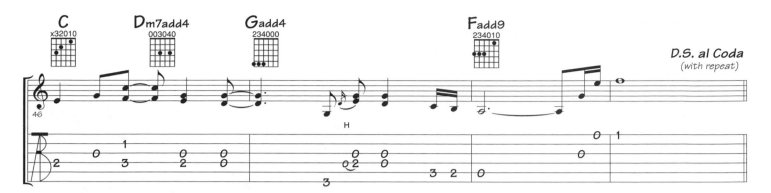

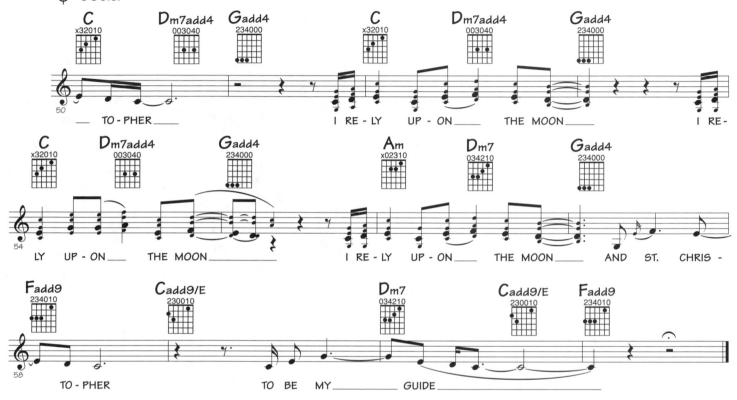

1. WHEN I WAS YOUNG I SPOKE LIKE A CHILD
    I SAW WITH A CHILD'S EYES
    AND AN OPEN DOOR WAS TO A GIRL
    LIKE THE STARS ARE TO THE SKY
    IT'S FUNNY HOW THE WORLD LIVES UP
    TO ALL YOUR EXPECTATIONS
    WITH ADVENTURES FOR THE STOUT OF HEART
    AND THE LURE OF THE OPEN SPACES

2. THERE'S TWO LANES RUNNING DOWN THIS ROAD
    WHICHEVER SIDE YOU'RE ON
    ACCOUNTS FOR WHERE YOU WANT TO GO
    OR WHAT YOU'RE RUNNING FROM
    BACK WHEN DARKNESS OVERTOOK ME
    ON A BLIND MAN'S CURVE

    I RELIED UPON THE MOON
    I RELIED UPON THE MOON
    I RELIED UPON THE MOON AND ST. CHRISTOPHER

3. NOW I'VE PAID MY DUES 'CAUSE I HAVE OWED THEM
    BUT I'VE PAID A PRICE SOMETIMES
    FOR BEING SUCH A STUBBORN WOMAN
    IN SUCH STUBBORN TIMES
    I'VE RUN FROM THE ARMS OF LOVERS
    I'VE RUN FROM THE EYES OF FRIENDS
    I HAVE RUN FROM THE HANDS OF KINDNESS
    I HAVE RUN JUST BECAUSE I CAN

4. BUT NOW I'VE GROWN AND I SPEAK LIKE A WOMAN
    AND I SEE WITH A WOMAN'S EYES
    AND AN OPEN DOOR IS TO ME NOW
    LIKE THE SADDEST OF GOOD-BYES
    WHEN IT'S TOO LATE FOR TURNING BACK
    I PRAY FOR THE HEART AND THE NERVE

    AND I RELY UPON THE MOON
    I RELY UPON THE MOON
    I RELY UPON THE MOON AND ST. CHRISTOPHER

    (Repeat Chorus)
    TO BE MY GUIDE

Paul Brady

Paul Brady first made his mark in the '60s and '70s playing traditional Irish music with the Johnstons, Planxty (which also featured soon-to-be luminaries Donal Lunny, Christy Moore, and Andy Irvine, with whom Brady performed as a duo from '76 to '78), and other bands. Toward the end of the '70s, Brady turned to solo albums and pop songwriting, and in the years since, artists as diverse as Tina Turner, Bonnie Raitt, Mary Black, and Art Garfunkel have covered his songs.

SELECTED DISCOGRAPHY

Nobody Knows . . . The Best of Paul Brady
Rykodisc 10491 (1999)

Andy Irvine and Paul Brady
Green Linnet 3006 (1981)
Green Linnet, 43 Beaver Brook Rd., Danbury, CT 06810;
(800) 468-6644; www.greenlinnet.com

Welcome Here Kind Stranger
Green Linnet 3015 (1978)

Arthur McBride

Traditional, arranged by Paul Brady

Paul Brady first recorded this haunting Irish ballad in 1976 on the classic album *Andy Irvine and Paul Brady.* This transcription comes from a very similar 1998 performance released on the retrospective *Nobody Knows . . . The Best of Paul Brady.* Long an admirer of Brady's music, Bob Dylan put his own twist on Brady's "Arthur McBride" on his 1992 album *Good As I Been to You.*

At the time he first recorded this tune, Brady was familiar with many versions of it from the '60s folk revival. His rendition is based

on a version printed in a book called *A Heritage of Songs: The Songs of Carrie Grover* (Grover was a woman from Maine with Scottish and Irish ancestry). In 1974, Brady debuted his arrangement with Planxty in Dublin, and it became one of the most popular songs of his career. His flatpicked guitar part on this seven-minute-plus masterpiece alternates between chordal accompaniment and melodic breaks between the song's many verses, making the most of the ringing strings available in open-G tuning.

—Jeffrey Pepper Rodgers

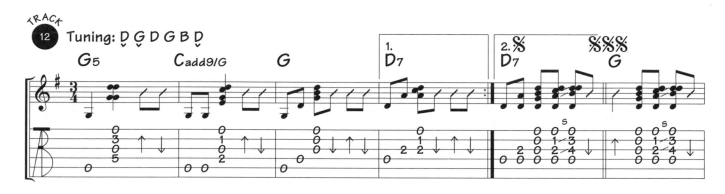

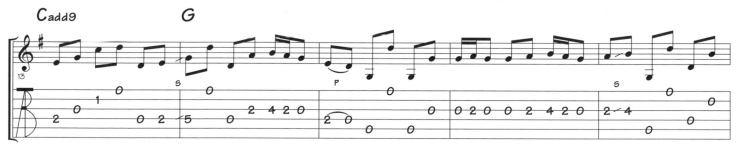

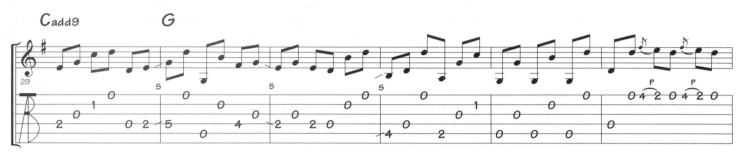

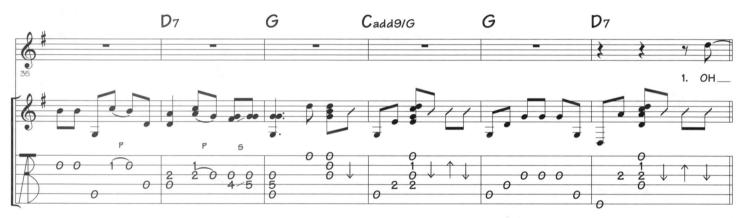

Verse

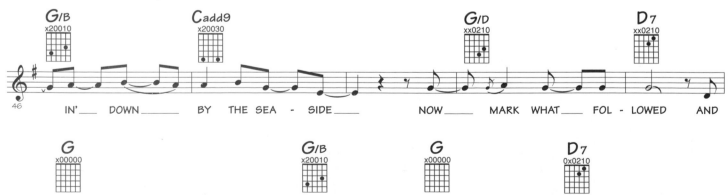

— ME AND ME COUS-IN ONE AR - THUR MC - BRIDE_____ AS WE_____ WENT_____ A - WALK -

2-8. *See additional lyrics.*

IN'___ DOWN_____ BY THE SEA - SIDE_____ NOW_____ MARK WHAT_____ FOL - LOWED AND

WHAT DID BE - TIDE_____ FOR IT BE - IN' ON____ CHRIST - MAS MORN - IN'____

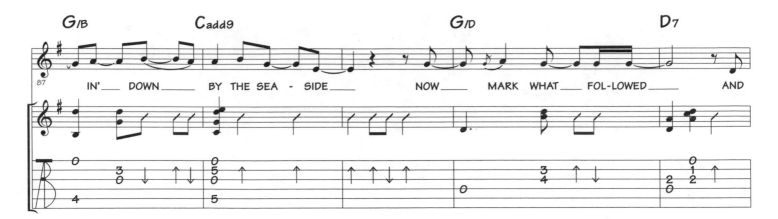

IN' ___ DOWN _____ BY THE SEA - SIDE ____ NOW _____ MARK WHAT ___ FOL-LOWED _____ AND

WHAT DID BE - TIDE _____ FOR IT BE - IN' ON ___ CHRIST - MAS ___ MORN - IN' ___

1. OH ME AND ME COUSIN ONE ARTHUR McBRIDE
   AS WE WENT A-WALKIN' DOWN BY THE SEASIDE
   NOW MARK WHAT FOLLOWED AND WHAT DID BETIDE
   FOR IT BEIN' ON CHRISTMAS MORNIN'
   OUT FOR RECREATION WE WENT ON A TRAMP
   AND WE MET SERGEANT NAPPER AND CORPORAL VAMP
   AND A LITTLE WEE DRUMMER INTENDING TO CAMP
   FOR THE DAY BEIN' PLEASANT AND CHARMIN'

2. "GOOD MORNIN' GOOD MORNIN'" THE SERGEANT DID CRY
   "AND THE SAME TO YOU GENTLEMEN" WE DID REPLY
   INTENDIN' NO HARM BUT MEANT TO PASS BY
   FOR IT BEIN' ON CHRISTMAS MORNIN'
   "BUT" SAYS HE "MY FINE FELLOWS, IF YOU WILL ENLIST
   IT'S TEN GUINEAS IN GOLD I WILL SLIP IN YOUR FIST
   AND A CROWN IN THE BARGAIN FOR TO KICK UP THE DUST
   AND DRINK THE KING'S HEALTH IN THE MORNIN'"

3. "FOR A SOLDIER HE LEADS A VERY FINE LIFE
   AND HE ALWAYS IS BLESSED WITH A CHARMING YOUNG WIFE
   AND HE PAYS ALL HIS DEBTS WITHOUT SORROW OR STRIFE
   AND ALWAYS LIVES PLEASANT AND CHARMIN'
   AND A SOLDIER HE ALWAYS IS DECENT AND CLEAN
   IN THE FINEST OF CLOTHIN' HE'S CONSTANTLY SEEN
   WHILE OTHER POOR FELLOWS GO DIRTY AND MEAN
   AND SUP ON THIN GRUEL IN THE MORNIN'"

4. "WELL" SAYS ARTHUR "I WOULDN'T BE PROUD OF YOUR CLOTHES
   FOR YOU'VE ONLY THE LEND OF THEM AS I SUPPOSE
   AND YOU DARE NOT CHANGE THEM ONE NIGHT FOR YOU KNOW
   IF YOU DO YOU'LL BE FLOGGED IN THE MORNIN'
   AND ALTHOUGH THAT WE ARE SINGLE AND FREE
   WE TAKE GREAT DELIGHT IN OUR OWN COMPANY
   AND WE HAVE NO DESIRE STRANGE FACES TO SEE
   ALTHOUGH THAT YOUR OFFERS ARE CHARMIN'"

5. "AND WE HAVE NO DESIRE TO TAKE YOUR ADVANCE
ALL HAZARDS AND DANGERS WE BARTER ON CHANCE
FOR YOU WOULD HAVE NO SCRUPLES TO SEND US TO FRANCE
WHERE WE WOULD GET SHOT WITHOUT WARNIN'

6. "OH NO" SAYS THE SERGEANT "I'LL HAVE NO SUCH CHAT
AND I NEITHER WILL TAKE IT FROM SPALPEEN OR BRAT
FOR IF YOU INSULT ME WITH ONE OTHER WORD
I'LL CUT OFF YOUR HEADS IN THE MORNIN'"
AND THEN ARTHUR AND I WE SOON DREW OUR HODS
AND WE SCARCE GAVE THEM TIME FOR TO DRAW THEIR
    OWN BLADES
WHEN A TRUSTY SHILLELAGH CAME OVER THEIR HEADS
AND BADE THEM TAKE THAT AS FAIR WARNING

7. AND THEIR OLD RUSTY RAPIERS THAT HUNG BY THEIR SIDE
WE FLUNG THEM AS FAR AS WE COULD IN THE TIDE
"NOW TAKE THEM OUT DEVILS" CRIED ARTHUR McBRIDE
"AND TEMPER THEIR EDGE IN THE MORNIN'"
AND THE LITTLE WEE DRUMMER WE FLATTENED HIS POW
AND WE MADE A FOOTBALL OF HIS ROWDY-DOW-DOW
THREW IT IN THE TIDE FOR TO ROCK AND TO ROW
AND BADE IT A TEDIOUS RETURNING

8. AND WE HAVIN' NO MONEY PAID THEM OFF IN CRACKS
AND WE PAID NO RESPECT TO THEIR TWO BLOODY BACKS
FOR WE LATHERED THEM THERE LIKE A PAIR OF WET SACKS
AND LEFT THEM FOR DEAD IN THE MORNIN'
AND SO TO CONCLUDE AND TO FINISH DISPUTES
WE OBLIGINGLY ASKED IF THEY WANTED RECRUITS
FOR WE WERE THE LADS WHO WOULD GIVE THEM HARD CLOUTS
AND BID THEM LOOK SHARP IN THE MORNIN'

9. OH ME AND ME COUSIN ONE ARTHUR McBRIDE
AS WE WENT A WALKIN' DOWN BY THE SEASIDE
NOW MARK WHAT FOLLOWED AND WHAT DID BETIDE
FOR IT BEIN' ON CHRISTMAS MORNIN'

Also Available in the *Acoustic Guitar* CD Songbook Series

From String Letter Publishing

Each title has a CD with original artist recordings plus a book with complete guitar transcriptions. All include songs in both standard and alternate tunings.

Rhythms of the Road

Bruce Cockburn • Toshi Reagon • Don Ross • Norman Blake • Kelly Joe Phelps • Cheryl Wheeler • Peter Mulvey • Dave Alvin • Steve James • Doc Watson • Eddie Lang • Jesse Winchester • Jesse Cook • Eliades Ochoa (CD-only bonus track) *(64 pp., $16.95, Item #21699229, ISBN 1-890490-17-2)*

Fingerstyle Guitar Masterpieces

Leo Kottke • Jorma Kaukonen • Peppino D'Agostino • Ed Gerhard • Adrian Legg • Chris Proctor • Martin Simpson • John Renbourn • John Williams • Duck Baker • Preston Reed • Jacques Stotzem *(72 pp., $16.95, Item #21699222, ISBN 1-890490-13-X)*

High on a Mountain

Steve Earle and the Del McCoury Band • Wayne Henderson • Beth Orton • Franco Morone • Nick Drake • Kate and Anna McGarrigle • Clive Gregson • Woody Mann • Gillian Welch • Jones and Leva • Andrew York • Taj Mahal • El McMeen • Judith Edelman • Jennifer Kimball *(72 pp., $16.95, Item #21699195, ISBN 1-890490-09-1)*

Habits of the Heart

Elliott Smith • Chris Whitley • David Grier • Guy Davis • Mike Dowling • Stephen Fearing • Laura Love • Josh White • Jerry Douglas • Merle Travis • Roy Rogers • Dan Bern • Kristin Hersh • Scott Tennant • Jim Croce *(64 pp., $16.95, Item #21699182, ISBN 1-890490-164)*

What Goes Around

Corey Harris • Mississippi John Hurt • Cats and Jammers • Bill Frisell • Muleskinner • Ricky Skaggs • Tom Russell • Edgar Meyer, Béla Fleck, and Mike Marshall • Dama • Patty Larkin • Paulo Bellinati • Janis Ian • Steve Tilston • D'Gary • Catie Curtis • Duncan Sheik *(72 pp., $16.95, Item #21699180, ISBN 1-890490-121)*

Acoustic Guitar Artist Songbook, Vol. 1

Sérgio Assad • Duck Baker • Doyle Dykes • Steve Earle* • Beppe Gambetta • Vince Gill • John Wesley Harding • Michael Hedges* • Philip Hii • Robyn Hitchcock • Jewel* • Pat Kirtley • Earl Klugh • Mike Marshall • Pat Metheny • Keb' Mo'* • Scott Nygaard • Pierce Pettis • Kelly Joe Phelps • Chris Proctor • Andrés Segovia • Martin Simpson • Tim Sparks • Jorge Strunz • Toru Takemitsu • Townes Van Zandt • Gillian Welch • Paul Yandell *(100 pp., 2 CDs, $29.95, Item #21699216, ISBN 1-890490-03-2)*
* Not included on CD

For more information on books from String Letter Publishing, or to place an order, please call Music Dispatch at (800) 637-2852, fax (414) 774-3259, or mail to Music Dispatch, PO Box 13920, Milwaukee, WI 53213. Visit String Letter Publishing on-line at www.stringletter.com.

CD track credits

1. **David Wilcox, "Eye of the Hurricane"** (David Wilcox). From *KBCO Studio C*, Vol. 9, KBCO 09 (1997). Recorded live at KBCO Studio C by Scott Arbough.

2. **CPR, "That House"** (David Crosby, Jeff Pevar, and James Raymond). From *CPR*, Samson 145 (1998). David Crosby, lead vocal, acoustic guitar; Jeff Pevar, vocals, acoustic guitar, electric slide guitar; James Raymond, vocals, piano; James "Hutch" Hutchinson, bass; Russ Kunkel, drums; Luis Conte, percussion. ℗ & © Gold Circle Entertainment, Inc.

3. **Sonny Chillingworth, "Moe 'Uhane (Dream Slack Key)"** (Sonny Chillingworth). From *Sonny Solo,* Dancing Cat/Windham Hill 38005 (1994). Courtesy of Dancing Cat Records (www.dancingcat.com).

4. **John Cephas and Phil Wiggins, "John Henry"** (traditional, arranged by John Cephas and Phil Wiggins). From *Dog Days of August,* Flying Fish/Rounder 70394 (1984). John Cephas, vocals and guitar; Phil Wiggins, harmonica. ℗ & © 1984 Rounder Records. Courtesy of Rounder Records.

5. **Ani DiFranco, "Cradle and All"** (Ani DiFranco). From *Not a Pretty Girl,* Righteous Babe 007 (1995). Ani DiFranco, vocals and acoustic, steel, electric, and bass guitars; Andy Stochansky, drums. ℗ 1995 Righteous Babe Records Inc.

6. **Alex de Grassi, "The Water Garden"** (Alex de Grassi). From *The Water Garden,* Tropo 1001 (1998). ℗ & © Tropo Records, PO Box 772, Redwood Valley, CA 95470.

7. **Dougie MacLean, "Caledonia"** (Dougie MacLean). From *Craigie Dhu,* Dunkeld 001 (1983). ℗ 1983 Dunkeld Records.

8. **Ledward Kaapana, "Whee Ha Swing"** (Sonny Chillingworth). From *Led Live,* Dancing Cat/Windham Hill 38008 (1994). Courtesy of Dancing Cat Records (www.dancingcat.com).

9. **Trian, "The Death of Queen Jane"** (lyrics traditional, music by Dáithí Sproule). From *Trian II,* Green Linnet 1159 (1995). Dáithí Sproule, vocals and guitar; Liz Carroll, fiddle; Billy McComiskey, accordion. ℗ & © 1995 Green Linnet Records, Inc.

10. **Peter Finger, "101 South"** (Peter Finger). From *Open Strings,* Acoustic Music 1173 (1999). © 1999 Sordino Musikverlag.

11. **Mary Chapin Carpenter, "The Moon and St. Christopher"** (Mary Chapin Carpenter). From *Shooting Straight in the Dark,* Columbia/Sony 46077 (1990). Mary Chapin Carpenter, vocals and acoustic guitar; John Jennings, background vocals and electric and acoustic guitars; Robbie Magruder, drums; Matt Rollings, piano; Rico Petrucelli, bass; Shawn Colvin, duet vocal. ℗ & © CBS Records Inc.

12. **Paul Brady, "Arthur McBride"** (traditional, arranged by Paul Brady). From *Nobody Knows: The Best of Paul Brady,* Rykodisc 10491 (1999). ℗ 1999 Abirgreen Ltd.